William Bell Scott

A Poet's Harvest Home

100 Short Poems

William Bell Scott

A Poet's Harvest Home
100 Short Poems

ISBN/EAN: 9783337006532

Printed in Europe, USA, Canada, Australia, Japan

Cover: Foto ©Thomas Meinert / pixelio.de

More available books at **www.hansebooks.com**

A Poet's Harvest Home:

Being One Hundred Short Poems

By WILLIAM BELL SCOTT, H.RSA., LLD.

WITH AN AFTERMATH

Of Twenty Short Poems

LONDON
ELKIN MATHEWS & JOHN LANE
THE BODLEY HEAD, VIGO STREET, W.
1893

A Poet's Harvest Home
(Fcap. 8vo., 156 pp.) 1882.

———

A Poet's Harvest Home
With an Aftermath
(Fcap. 8vo., 196 pp.) 1893.

Stories such as soothfast were,
If they be said in good manner,
Have double pleasance in the carping.
Pleasance first is in the harping,
The second in the soothfasiness,
That shows the thing just as it was.

BARBOUR.

TO

W. M. ROSSETTI

THESE RECORDS OF A SEASON

ARE INSCRIBED

IN MEMORY OF THE FRIENDSHIP

OF HALF A LIFETIME.

CONTENTS.

viii CONTENTS.

CONTENTS.

OF POETRY.

OF POETS.

CONTENTS.

Those marked with an asterisk (*) in the above Index have been interpolated, and are of earlier years.

AN AFTERMATH.

POEMS.

PROLOGUE.

LITTLE dear ! we often say
To bright young eyes and dainty ears :
The two words oft together go,
     Would I could know
Together they might go to-day,
And designate in coming years,
These my verses—rather small,
I hope, to weary or appal—
Small as drops of blood or tears.

' Pretty if good !' grand-dame replied
To the vain youngster by her side :
' Good if true,' it seems to me,
Our verses should be judged to be :
If nature prompts, not merely art :
Only emotion's potent spell
Can clothe life with the lovely shell,
And send the rhyme like love's own dart
Flying direct from heart to heart.
Ah me ! then, reader, can you say
' Little dears' to these to-day ?

SMOOTHED by this untiring tide,
 The rocks that crop up on this strand
Make pleasant seats, we there abide,
 And spread our white cloth on the sand.

'Twas such a gentle sea, none there
 Could ever after quite forget,
Sea-mews sloped near us through warm air,
 The small white cloudlets made a fret,
High, higher still, like Jacob's stair.

What do they now in ancient Rome,—
 Where we were looked for certainly,
We chose this year to stay at home,
 And lay the stale schoolmaster bye.

'Art is something more than nature,'
 Something from the artist's life,
Life orders and selects, makes sure,
 Frees the melody from strife.

4

But that life lapses 'neath the sway
  Of motives long since past and gone;
Beautiful once, they had their day,
  We look for bread and find a stone.

Let the pulse beat: a verse or two
  May come from this kind solitude,
By sea, in bower, 'neath cloud, or blue,
  To fit our manhood's present mood.

THE FOXGLOVE.

A REMINISCENCE OF THE WAR 1870.

I.

THAT foxglove by the garden gate,
   The very day the war began,
Opened its first, its lowest flower.
  The post that morn was late;
Anxious I waited for the man,
Then went into this wild-rose bower,
And heard the warning voice of fate.

Week by week, even day by day,
Another petal opened fair,
Advancing up the long light stem:
      I counted them,
        As I passed there,
While my heart was far away,
Listening early, listening late,
To the German march-- the march of Fate
     And when France lay
Quivering in the gory day,
      The topmost bell
Rang a dirge before it fell

THE FOXGLOVE.

II.

OFT throughout that deadly fight,
  We owned that might was right.
For from the step of the Madeleine,
Amid the trumpets' loud fanfare,
Years long ago we had seen there
Louis, triumphant from the South,
Hailed by the brutal popular mouth ;
Through the streets where late the stain
Of blood lay did his triumph fare.
      I heard the cheer;
While many said the day must come,
When, God with us, right shall be might.
Behold ! with cannon, trump, and drum
      Now was it here !
      The span of time
A foxglove bloom its stalk might climb,
He passed for ever from our sight.

BUT what have wars or kings to do
　　With our quiet country ways,
Or with poetry now-a-days ?
The Foxglove by the gate that grew
Brought them to mind, and made me lose
Myself in that past stream of news :
And there it still remains to-day ;
The Mistress of our Garden Bower
Caring for each wild blossoming
The summer months successive bring.

Each morning here, in sun or shower,
Awhile we sit while I rehearse,
As matin service, some new lay,
　　　　Some little verse,
Various as this sea-side weather,
Or that hill-side rough with heather,
Rhyme-children of the transient hour,
Records perchance of yesterday,
　　　Or tales from twilights far away.

3

THE ROBIN.

CRUMBS for the robin; well he knew
    The click of that old garden gate,
Among the leaves he somewhere flew,
    Nor came to breakfast ever late.

From twig to twig he ventures near,
    With sidelong bright dark eye he comes,
Not for the poems but the crumbs:
    We take good care he need not fear.

Is that the garden gate again?
    Comes the maid to gather peas?
It is the gardener, well-known swain:
    Our robin likes old friends like these.

But hark! that click once more, we see
    A caller feathered for the day,
He knows as well, it seems, as we
    The time is come to fly away.

CONTENT.

YESTREEN I heard a child's faint cry,
  'Where is Phemie, Phemie Blayne?'
As I with book in hand passed by—
  Call louder, child, oh, call again.

The infant did, it shrieked amain,
  'Annie Logie, where is she?'
A sweeter name than Phemie Blayne!
  Where can the loitering damsels be?

Annie Logie, Phemie Blayne!
  Good heavens, could I only see
Their innocent faces, they might sain
  And save poor thought-distempered me.

In that thatched cottage to remain,
  Phemie Blayne to woo and wed,
  Or Annie Logie choose instead!
Were I but twenty-one again,
  With no ambitions in my head!

' MISTRESS, here is Phemie Blayne
    Selling mushrooms once again ;
Annie Logie came before
You had passed your chamber door,
So I filled the basket there—'

Mushrooms ! Phemie Blayne ! oh where ?
With that I ran pell-mell down stair.
This was but trifling to restore
The interest of the day before,—
        But there she stood,
Clothed in her beauty, plainly good.
Upon her auburn hair a hood,
Coarse perhaps, but white as milk,
Neater than the finest silk :
Tall and elastic, strong and free,
Like a blossoming apple-tree,
Earnest-eyed and womanly,
Yet little more than child to-day,
There stood she waiting patiently.

Phemie Blayne ! I still can see
Thy queenhood, humbling then to me,
And wonder if thy destiny
Is good as God has been to thee.

THE children in their best at last
    Were gathered on the lawn,
By sex divided, or by ages classed;
Had nuts or oranges, then lists were drawn
    For leaping, running, and the rest ;
    Some did right well, but Willie best.
    At first the taller girls were shy
    Against the boys their powers to try,
But whispering long, together cling,
    Till their little scheme is planned,
When down they sit in one wide ring,
While one by lot selected stood,
    In her hand her neat white hood.
Then out and in, the circle round
    Stepping, she began to sing :
      ' I writ a letter to my love,
      ' And on the way I dropt it,
      ' I carried it within my glove,
      ' But still and still I dropt it,
      ' I dropt, I dropt—'

Then suddenly she stopt,
Amidst the bright clear faces crowned
With expectation shining round,
And all the little ready feet
Ready to jump up to meet
The hood when it was thrown !
The game was then to run so fast,
To o'ertake her the hood had cast,
But who already far had flown,
In and about, and round and round
All the bright faces on the ground.

Another of these innocent games
Perplexed us, although much we tried
To understand the joyous claims
Its rhymes denied.
 'Rise, sister Sally, now, rise if you can,
 'Rise, sister Sally, and choose a young man;
 'Choose to the east and choose to the west,
 'And choose out the very one you can love best.'
After this song we scarce could tell
How many changes there befell,
With dancing left and dancing right,
And singing thus with all their might:

' *Now you are married, ay, married in joy,*
' *First for a girl and next for a boy;*
' *Seven years long enough, seven years, oh ho,*
' *Now the play's played out, kiss, kiss, and go, go.'*
With milk and cake, as well as game,
They had enough when evening came,
And sunset gilt each dainty head,
    Showing time to go to bed.
  So with another wild huzzay,
Their banners waved them all away.

About Glenkindie and his man,
A false ballant hath long been writ;
Some bootless loon had written it,
 Upon a bootless plan :
 But I have found the true at last,
And here it is, so hold it fast.
'Twas made by a kind damozel
Who loved him and his man right well.

G LENKINDIE, best of harpers, came
 Unbidden to our town,
And he was sad and sad to see,
 For love had worn him down.

It was the love, as all men know,
 The love that brought him down
The hopeless love for the king's daughter
 The dove that heired a crown.

GLENKINDIE.

Now he wore not that collar of gold,
 His dress was forest green,
His wondrous fair and rich mantel
 Had lost its silvery sheen.

But still by his side walked Rafe, his boy,
 In goodly cramoisie,
Of all the boys that ever I saw,
 The goodliest boy was he.

Oh, Rafe the page, oh Rafe the page,
 Ye stole the heart frae me ;
Oh, Rafe the page, oh Rafe the page,
 I wonder where ye be ;
We ne'er may see Glenkindie more,
 But may we never see thee ?

Glenkindie came within the hall,
 We set him on the dais,
And gave him bread, and gave him wine,
 The best in all the place.

We set for him the guest's high chair,
 And spread the naperie,
Our Dame herself would serve for him,
 And I for Rafe, perdie !

GLENKINDIE.

But down he sat on a low, low stool,
  And thrust his long legs out,
And leant his back to the high chair,
  And turned his harp about.

He turned it round, he stroked the strings,
  He touched each tirling-pin,
He put his mouth to the sounding-board
  And breathed his breath therein.

And Rafe sat over against his face,
  And looked at him wistfullie,
I almost grat ere he began,
  They were so sad to see.

The very first stroke he strack that day
  We all came crowding near,
And the second stroke he strack that day
  We all were smit with fear.

The third stroke that he strack that day
  Full fain we were to cry,
The fourth stroke that he strack that day
  We thought that we would die.

GLENKINDIE.

No tongue can tell how sweet it was,
  How far and yet how near,
We saw the saints in Paradise,
  And bairnies on their bier.

And our sweet Dame saw her good lord
  She told me privilie—
She saw him as she saw him last,
  On his ship upon the sea.

Anon he laid his little harp by,
  He shut his wondrous eyes,
We stood a long time like dumb things,
  Stood in a dumb surprise.

Then all at once we left that trance,
  And shouted where we stood,
We clasped each other's hands and vowed
  We would be wise and good.

Soon he rose up and Rafe rose too,
  He drank wine and broke bread,
He clasped hands with our trembling Dame,
  But never a word he said.
They went, alack and lack-a-day,
  They went the way they came.

I followed them all down the floor,
 And oh but I had drouth,
To touch his cheek, to touch his hand,
 To kiss Rafe's velvet mouth.

But I knew such was not for me :
 They went straight from the door ;
We saw them fade within the mist,
 And never saw them more.

ONCE on a time, as stories tell,
　　Teliessin, Cymric master-bard,
Leant o'er the fire in the bardic hall,
Thinking of the ills that fall
On a small people nigh a great ;
Ills waxen measureless of late,
Since his master's passing bell
Passed the mountain road so hard ;
The road to an untimely grave,
Untimely to the good and brave.

The dying embers flickered down,
In from the night dry leaves had blown,
When a faint sound his ear doth greet,
That makes him rise upon his feet.
Was it the disused wires that rung,
Of some old harp by night-wind swung,
Within this bardic cloister hung ?
It was not wind, no blasts now blow,
But gently first, and sweetly slow,

His master's harp from that high wall,
Preluded, rose to battle call,
Then changed by moaning fainting fall
Into the dirge wherewith the bard
Passed that mountain road so hard.

Teliessin turned, but nought could see,
Cried out,—'Come, Master, come to me !'
A strange, far-off dear voice replied,
'Come thou, come over to this side:
There are harpers brave and good
In the heart of God's great wood :
Son Teliessin, come away.'
  ' Master dear,' the young man cried,
  'I am ready, show the way !'

   This was the day
Ten years ago the master died;
This was the darkening hour also,
Teliessin left both friend and foe.
Nor ever from that night agen
Hath he been seen by mortal men.

HELP.

WHEN the portly monk would ride,

Upon his patron-saint he cried

For help, if the good saint inclined,

This once to be so kind.

Then with a long and strong essay,

He rose in such a vigorous way,

As sent him over t' other side.

He rubbed his shin, set straight his hood,

And to his saint again he cried,

Worse and worse ! you 're over good,

I always like to stop half way !

24

OISIN.

OISIN, son of great Fingal,
Of Fenian race the last of all,
Longed to see his native land
With longing nothing could withstand.

An hundred years ago and more,
He had left old Erin's shore,
On the winged white horse astride,
Left in the mists that all things hide,
With the strange princess in his arms,
Left for the realm beyond all harms,
Beyond the moon, beyond the sea,
Unknown to bards of best degree,
Where the sword was never tried,
Where they were neither born nor died ;
The realm of Youth, youth ever more.
With years the longing grew apace,

The nameless princess by his side,
Loving and lovely, limb and face,
  Tall and bright as is the flame,
That lights the witches' deeds of shame,
  Beautiful and filled with pride,
  Such as no bard can express
Who knows not the wild leopardess ;
But he left and hither came.
'Dismount not from thy winged white horse,
  See old Erin and come back,
Dismount not or it will be worse
Than I can tell thee, worse, alack !'
She signed him on his eye and ear
With water from the Wells of Fear,
  And the wingéd courser bore
  Oisin to old Erin's shore.

Erin, land of my desire,
Land of my childhood and my sire !
He cried as on the horse he sat,
  *Agadsa, ataim agat !**

* 'With thee, I am with thee,' in the ancient Irish.

His eyes at first so filled with tears,
  Scarce saw he, but soon wept aloud,
    It went beyond his fears ;
    There was no Tara left at all,
    There was no bard, no harp, no hall,
    But tonsured pigmies in a crowd,
    Were building bell-towers everywhere.
      Erin, land beyond all peers,
      Erin, land of my desire,
Woe's me, thou hast not passed the fire
As I have done, the fire of years :
Oisin's tears were salt indeed
Sitting upon the winged white steed.
Alas, the pigmies by his side,
Struggling to raise a lintel-stone,
Began to tremble, and to moan,
Down he leapt with kindly speed,
At once, his strength was gone, his hair
Was snow-white, he bent trembling there,
He touched old Erin's ground and died.

THESE froward waves, we feign they try
   To utter to us some mystery :
Such is the euphuistic game
We baffled poets follow.
Pantheistic ? All the same,
Like the sounding cymbal hollow :—
We it is and not the sea
Long to speak out God's mystery :
Immense and world-old salt ocean,
With thy moon-adoring motion,
   Thou hast nought to us to say,
   We must speak and thou obey.

OBLIVIOUSLY we long sat there
    Weaving lines to praise the sea,
Objecting still, we still compare,
And try to make the rhythm agree
Between the verses and the sea.
When we thus began, the wave
Drove the pebbles up the beach,
Then resilient to the main
Drew them with it back again :
Nor dreamt we where the tide might reach,
Till it was round us everywhere,
Deep enough to be our grave !
For this is still the destined way,
We are the masters, yet the prey.

AT SEA.

N OW the tide is safe and high,
    In the fresh'ning morning breeze,
Over the harbour bar we hie
Out into the open seas.

With these fisher lads so strong
And knowing in the water ways,
I'll try to make a summer song,
The fisher's summer life to praise.

It seems to me the rounded sea
Begins to swell above the shore,
And the great gull, that fisher free,
Dives right down a yard or more.

With main and jib we bound along,
Through showers of spray we rise and dip,
But as for making any song,
That needs a sea apprenticeship.

And now we meet the ocean swell,
The bow swings high up in the air ;
My breath goes with it !   I know well
The land is best for me, not there !

We islanders should love the sea,
The fresh wind, coiled nets, ballast heap,
And full brown sail ; but as for me,
Again within that harbour's lee,
I let the sea-song go to sleep !

THE HURRICANE.

THIS morn the wind flew through the trees
 Like a flock of driven game,
And as the morning passed to noon
 It waxed into a raving flame.

These fisher lads that yesterday
 Rowed us to the fresh green sea,
Said they were bound to start betimes,
 For whitings round by Ailsa's lee.

Heaven help them in this furious gale;
 I'll make my way down to the strand,
And see if both friends, Rob and Will,
 Have got safe back to wife and land.

It was no easy thing to do,
 To struggle with the gale to-day,
To struggle and conquer, one strong man,
 Buttoned up on firm foot-way.

But down upon the quay the surf
 Flew, blinding eyes and over head,
And there amidst the coil I found
 Little Effie wild with dread.

She could not hear, I could not speak,
   The roaring of the winds forbade,
So there I made her cling to me,
   And this is what may now be said.

Her hood was gone, her loosened hair
   Shot round us like a tangled net,
But still she stared across the bar
   Through blinding locks and blind seafret.

For there she knew the boat, my God !
   Where Robin rowed and Willie steered,
Between the grey wall and the bay,
   With spray and mist obscurely bleared.

Ah ! will they do it, can it live,—
   Their coble in that hurricane,
Rocks below and walls to face ?
   Effie wiped her eyes in pain,
But still I thought she could not see,
   She wiped them, wiped them yet again.

Is it over, has it mounted in ?
   Yes, yes, oh, little Effie, now
Let me wipe your eyes once more,
   Willie knows you from the prow.

D—2   33

THE NORNS WATERING YGGDRASILL.

(FOR A PICTURE.)

WITHIN the unchanging twilight
　　Of the high land of the gods,
Between the murmuring fountain
　　And the Ash-tree, tree of trees,
The Norns, the terrible maidens,
　　For evermore come and go.

Yggdrasill the populous Ash-tree,
　　Whose leaves embroider heaven,
Fills all the grey air with music—
　　To Gods and to men sweet sounds
But speech to the fine-eared maidens
　　Who evermore come and go.

That way to their doomstead thrones
   The Aesir ride each day,
And every one bends to the saddle
   As they pass beneath the shade ;
Even Odin, the strong All-father,
Bends to the beautiful maidens
   Who cease not to come and go.

The tempest crosses the high boughs,
   The great snakes heave below,
The wolf, the boar, and antlered harts
   Delve at the life-giving roots,
But all of them fear the wise maidens,
The wise-hearted water-bearers
   Who evermore come and go.

And men far away, in the night-hours
   To the north-wind listening, hear,
They hear the howl of the were-wolf,

And know he hath felt the sting
Of the eyes of the potent maidens
  Who sleeplessly come and go.

They hear on the wings of the north wind
  A sound as of three that sing,
And the skald, in the blae mist wandering
  High on the midland fell,
Heard the very words of the o'ersong
  Of the Norns who come and go.

But alas for the ears of mortals
  Chance-hearing that fate-laden song !
The bones of the skald lie there still,—
  For the speech of the leaves of the Tree
Is the song of the three Queen-maidens
  Who evermore come and go.

WOULD you be free of a salt-sea grave,
    Drink from your palm of the high tenth wave,
Eat of the yew the topmost leaf,
And the midmost cornhead out of the sheaf,
Bind a rune around each arm ;
Then you need fear no salt-sea harm.
Thorolf, stark and large of bone,
Must whet his sword, his casque must don,
And leave long-haired Gudrun alone :
Thorolf did all these and more,
He threw the live brand from the door,
They clasped hands through the thorough stone,
Three kisses kissed, and he was gone.

Gudrun ascends to her own bower,
The highest chamber in the tower :
She opens the small shot-window
That she may see the great ships go,
Far away and far below :

Now they come, the wide wings set
That all the southern gale be met ;
The first was large, the sails were red,
With the black raven on them spread,
In that the first, so proud, so fair,
My love and all his men must fare ;
Another, more grand still, comes on,
My lover's sure must be that one—
But a larger dragon still
Quits the shadow of the hill ;
Oh, I must learn each name to call,
And make charmed runes for each and all.

Round by Lessoe's broken strand,
Out by Elsinore's white sand,
They ride the dark-green ocean free,
Straight westward to the English sea,
With heavy brand and grasping hand
They swoop down on nord-Humber land.

And now the green cloth, red cloth rare,
He wins Gudrun to shape and wear,
A golden tire for her light hair

When the bower-maidens braid it tight,
After the marriage day and night;
Many a gift to hang in hall,
And great carved chest to hold them all.

On they pass from shore to shore,
But runners fleet have fled before;
Mascled breast, mailed hand and knee,
Gather within the high mole's lee.
Ah, wide-winged Hugin now flies past
To Valhall's high wall bound so fast:
Were I a true skald, I could see
The fate-dealing Damsels, three by three,
Fold up their sleeves, beneath each heart
Tighten their girdles, and depart.

———————

Gudrun, Gudrun, look out again,
Look over that far stormy main,
Dost thou see them three by three,
Flying towards the Scottish sea?
Second sight is not for thee,

But dost thou see
These ships returning to our bay,
And every man who went away,
Proud with the spoils of his sword-play,
Leaping from their prows this day?
　　Nay, far away,
With rolled-up sleeves these Doomsters grey,
Fly over heads of struggling men.
Men struggling in the deadly fray,
And again and yet again,
Like hungry eagles, birds of prey,
　　They stoop
And mark the heads that death shall coop.
　　Gudrun, to-day
The arrows fly and some must die,
The spears' thrust levelled to the heart,
No sword can waive their deadly smart.
Will Thorolf safe that deck regain,
Or is he coiled among the slain?
Gudrun, Gudrun, look out again—
But now the thick white smoke is blown
From those high ships where men are mown:
The mist comes over heart and brain.

Bleach, oh bleach, my white linen,
  Bleach, oh bleach, my grey,
I too am bleaching white and thin,
It is a year, a year to-day,—
Why doth Thorolf stay away?
  Why doth Thorolf stay?

That and this were for my bed,
  Yon was on the board to lay,
This to make my bower glad,
  And that was for embroidery.
Bleach, oh bleach, my white linen,
  Bleach, oh bleach, my grey,
I too am bleaching white and thin,
  Why doth Thorolf stay?

Summer went and autumn rose,
  Autumn passed with moaning gale,
Long winter followed with its close
  Of wandering tempest, icy hail.
Bleach, oh bleach, my white linen,
  Bleach, oh bleach, my grey,
I too am bleaching white and thin,
  Why doth my Thorolf stay?

Now spring, long waited for, at last
  Alone thou comest back to me,
My empty arms abroad I cast
  As I sit on this bleaching lea :
My eyes are failing, I scarce see
  The linen lying on the lea.
But what's my linen now to me ?
Few yards can wind a wasted May,
It is a year, a year to-day,
Why doth Thorolf stay away ?
  Why doth Thorolf stay ?

'YOUNG Loves to sell!' a voice calls out
    Beneath the trees, 'Young loves to sell!'
From porch and garden round about,
Child, maid, and matron hasten out—
The voice was like a silver bell,
    'Young loves to sell!'

She took the basket from her head,
This cunning nymph of Arcadie—
'Look at the soft wings, grey and red,
Fluttering in their pleachen bed,
Who 'll buy?   I will not wait, you see,
    Who 'll come to me?'

'Young loves to sell!'   The children run
About her, 'O take all our toys,
Take all we have and give us one!'
Old Laia spinning in the sun
Cries, 'Long since lost I all my joys,
    Give me but one!'

'Young loves to sell! I will not stay,
So maidens, maidens, come and buy,
I cannot give them without pay,
Nor let them fly; I 'll go away,
If no one quickly comes to try
　　　If she can buy.

'See how each little rosy dear
Smiles through the wicker bars at you,
Do not let your faint hearts fear
My darling loves, they smile and peer,
And this one, with wings azure blue,
　　　He beckons you.'

Silvia, where is Silvia hid?—
She loosed the pearling from her hair,
Her golden necklace she undid,
Her bracelet from her wrist she slid,
And ran and caught the prize so rare,
　　　Silvia the fair.

44

Then every one, and all at once,
Struggling round the wise nymph flew,
None would rest without a chance,
Such shining eyes and such a dance!
But Silvia's prettiest was I knew,
　　Wings azure blue!

THAT long-winged boy is sure to prate,
 So forward and so sly,
He grows too great, 'tis quite too late
To have him peep and pry.

He never leaves our sight, he's here
 And there and everywhere,
A listening ear for ever near
 We will no longer bear.

We must fall on him might and main,
 Bridget and I and you,
But don't be cruel, naughty Jane,
 Don't kiss him, silly Prue !

We 'll set him in the stocks and go,
 We 'll lock him fast all day,
But we may let him keep his bow—
 The child must have his play.

Thus did they, and with laughter great,
 Their game was well begun,
Alas ; ere they had shut the gate,
 He pinked them every one.

L ISTLESS the silent ladies sit
        About the room so gaily lit ;
Madame Ions likes the cups or tray,
But thinks it scarce enough to say :
Mistress Cox is gone astray
To the night-light in her own nursery,
Wonders if little Maude was led
Without long coaxing into bed :
Miss Jemima Applewhite,
On a low stool by the fire,
Concentrates her confused desire,—
Perhaps will do so all the night,
On an unused rhyme for ' scan,'
And can but find the stiff word *man* :
Miss Temple pets the little hound,
That has a tendency to whine,
To-night its cushion can't be found ;
And wonders when they'll leave the wine
Few take, but which men still combine
To linger over when they dine.

Indeed a frightful interval !
Madame Ions wants her game,
Or she must have her usual wink ;
But now satiric Bertha Stahl
Jumps upon the music-stool,
And breaks into a sportive flame ;
But what of all things do you think
She plays, that laughter-loving fool ?
The funeral march, Dead March of Saul !

Oh, Lord of Hosts ! their mailéd tread,
Bearing along the mailéd dead,
Makes me bow my stubborn head.
Never underneath the sun
Will this heart-fathoming march be done ;
Still, Lord of Hosts ! to thee we cry,
When our great ones, loved ones, die,
Still some grand lament we crave,
When we descend into the grave.

I turn, afraid that I may weep,—
Jemima's pestered wits still ran
After the unused rhyme for ' scan,'
Dear old Ions was asleep.

THE OLD OLD STORY.

I.

IT seems but yesterday, and yet
  I was then but two years from school,
This picture I can not forget,
Over all life's seething pool.
The sweet light voice, a living lute,
The sweet slim figure struck me mute ;
Matilda was the lovely name,
Within a neat red-pencilled frame
I wrote it in my first verse book,
Snugly kept in secret nook !

She came to us beneath the wing
Of her mamma, whose bonnet wide
Was an epitome of spring,—
So long since, I must even confide,
The great scooped bonnet was just then
Adored by fashion and by men :

Well I remember wondering
How this frank angel ever came
From such a broad-winged pompous dame !

And after forty years depart,
Child and mamma drop on us here ;
Can the slim figure and light heart
Beneath the same broad wing appear
Again in this far distant year ?
Ah no ! the ladies seem the same,
But the bonnet is quite different ;
Matilda is the pompous dame,
And this her daughter Millicent !

Good heavens ! it is indeed just so.
Time reproduces all his toys ;
Here is the pair of long ago
Touching the hearts of other boys.
And am I then to moralise,
With satire in my rhymes and eyes ?
The sonsy matron ! suppose we
Ask *her* now what she thinks of *me* ?

II.

I WOULD indeed like well to see
　What Matilda thinks, or thought of me
In that romantic early year
When her fine name I held so dear,
Or at least made it so appear
In my long-hid first verses book :
I'll try to wile her out to look
At the sundial or the bees,
And underneath the quivering trees
I shall touch on ancient things,
That so long since lost all their wings,
Or rather, to tell truth, I'd say,
Used them long since to fly away.
I did at once, and I must own
A faintly sentimental tone
Stole o'er my reminiscences,
As we passed, repassed the bees :
I said her child recalled her so,—
Revived in me the long ago—
The age was just about the same
When we once played a charming game,

Now quite gone out, upon the grass ;
And here again the bees we pass ;
Though she forgets to turn her head,
She answers in a cheerful mood,
Her daughter is both fair and good.
The gravel crunched beneath her tread
While she went on, and thus she said :

'Your memory's good for long ago,
I often wish that mine were so,
But when a girl is wed like me,
And carried quite away to town,
The rest soon fades away, you see :
The birds gone, soon the nest blows down :
Your brother James, now gone, and I
Had some flirtations certainly,
He was the red-haired one and tall :—
I can't remember you at all !'

I made reply, some sidelong mutter ;
We turned, we joined the rest at tea,
She ate three folds of bread and butter,
She had *never* thought at all of me !

THE APPLE TREE.

L ET us lie upon the grass
　　　Beneath this apple-tree,
To mark the shining white clouds pass,
Sailing in the high blue sea,
Through the net-work overhead
Of boughs and stems so thickly spread,
Flickering in the sunlit sheen,
　　　Of yellow and green,
With apples clustered everywhere.
　　　And now a bird
Darts into its nest up there ;
We are neither seen nor heard,
But each callow little bill
　　　Full well it knows,
　　　And each must fill,
So off and away again it goes,
While we lie upon the grass,
　　　Idle as we can be,
Watching only what may pass
　　　Within this apple tree.

WHAT sound was there?
　　　An apple fallen, I declare,
Ripe and red, and we will share,
As we have shared so much beside :
　　　No ! let it stay,
It makes me think of mistress Eve,
　　　And something might betide ;
What if we too should have to grieve
The loss of this our paradise !—
　　　But I've heard say,
From good Saint Jerome's comment wise,
　　　Eve was away　　　　　　`
When God did that commandment leave,
And therefore innocent was Eve :
Besides, no Snake is here to-day.

APPLE GATHERING.

THIS morn brought tedious news express,
    To master which in quietness,
As soon as might be I had clomb
To the room I sometimes call my home.
I may confess that pawns or kings
On the chessboard of church or court,
Bring me nor interest nor sport ;
Another kind of value clings
About the daily sheet for me,
An interest of a vulgar sort.

But then that child we call the gnome
Knocked with both small fists and cried,
    ' Theta is in the apple-tree,
     We are gathering, come and see ! '
I felt that I could not be spared,
And forthwith to the orchard fared,
    And soon descried
Theta's skirts of dusky red
Amidst the boughs, against the sky :
Janet too, both mounted there
This annual festival to share.

The boughs with dark-brown leaves o'erspread,
And crimsoned fruit ; the sky pure white,
With dense blue clefts that look so high,
Everything so sharp and bright,
Made up a picture chased outright
My tiresome news ; besides, in joy,
The happy household voices too,
That touch the heart, a welcome threw
About me, and the rich dull sound
Of apples dropping on the ground
Brought out the laughter of the boy.
Great piled-up baskets stood about :
' How shall we ever eat all these ? '
They seemed to him quite infinite—
' I too would pluck some if I might ! '
He clapped his hands, ' Oh let me, please !'
So I raised him over shoulder high,
The reddest, ripest, bunches nigh.
He caught them with a childish shout.
He was much merrier than was I
When I returned to read and write.

A BIRTHDAY.

IS this indeed All-Hallow's day,
When fairies hold their annual play?
As out of school like bees they fly,
I hear the village children cry
Upon the faery folk, brown, red,
Pink, green and blue, to go to bed.
All the faeries that were seen
At dawn upon the parson's green.
Then, dear, this is your natal day,
They may be more than usual gay
In their traditional array.
                But sad to say,
I have no gift to bring to you,
I had forgot this best of days
Until I heard the children's lays!
                But then 'tis true,
Being yours, it is my birth-day too,
My second birth—this best of days.

BEFORE MARRIAGE.

(THE WIFE SPEAKS.)

CAN you recall the life we led
   Before our meeting-day,
The day that we were wed
     As I may say?
     I often do,
    And wish I knew
If it is the same with you.
I was not sad, I was not gay,
It was my lifetime clad in grey:
A continuous December,
     As I remember,
Looking out for Christmas-day,
Like a child for cakes and play,
     With my brother,
     And my mother,
And my sisters in a row:
We were sheltered from the snow,
I was happy in a way,
Before that blessed waking day,
But now my life's bound up with thine,
You're my perennial cakes and wine.

TO THE DEAD.

(A PARAPHRASE.)

GONE art thou? gone, and is the light of day
    Still shining, is my hair not touched with
      grey?
But evening draweth nigh, I pass the door,
And see thee walking on the dim-lit shore.

Gone, art thou? gone, and weary on the brink
Of Lethe waiting there.   O do not drink,
Drink not, forget not, wait a little while,
I shall be with thee ; we again may smile.

ELIJAH.

THE widow heard Elijah's tread,
  She heard his staff against the door,
She wrapped the sackcloth round her head,
She took the small corpse from the bed
And sternly stood his face before.

Silent, as sleep-walking man,
He lifted from her breast the child,
And shut in his own cell began,
With tears that down his long beard ran,
The mystery,—God reconciled.

Mouth to mouth he gave the breath,
  Eyes to eyes he gave the sight,
Limb to limb,—the child beneath
Quivered and began to breathe—
  Trembled, cried out as in fright.

The mother hears outside the door,
Her one child is no longer dead,
She throws the sackcloth from her head,
She stumbles fainting on the floor,—
Lift the infant from the bed,
Let him his mother's life restore !

'OPEN the door ! Thou canst not understand
My mission, thou spoilt child of many a god,
Thou who dost claim the heart for thy abode ;
Open the door, lest I put forth my hand
And touch thee too, or give such dire command
  To thy vile brother, Hatred,—now I hear
  The quills of thy unquiet wings with fear
Quiver against thy flanks : no more withstand.'

'Oh Death, why comest thou so soon so far?
  Why comest thou before the appointed hour ?
I shall not make way for a fate so dire.'
' Poor child, I pass despite thy bolt and bar,
  The torch lit here to grace the bridal bower
I make it mine to light the funeral pyre.'

THE OFFERING.

AFTER THE ANTIQUE.

HERA, Athene, Cypria, great three,
Take these for all your care of me :—
A golden garland fair,
My longest braid of hair,
My bridal zone so rare.
Small gifts are these to represent
The ten years' guerdons ye have sent,—
A husband loved and sure,
A peaceful life and pure,
Male children on the floor.

BY Bacchus, no !
   Good Bacchus, be not slow
To keep them back beyond the floe
Of Danube's waters, where the snow
   Bites at the toe :
Good Bacchus, wine, thy gift, I know
Before I drink it, like the rose
That over leagues of India grows ;
I scent from far, but here my nose
Rebels and fancies he-goats ; well !
These Kelts that live among our foes
Take corn for grapes, and with some spell
Corrupting it, make this strong drink—
   But stay, I think
The potion makes my senses blink !

THE CANDIDATE.

AFTER THE ANTIQUE.

LIGHT-GIRDED Phœbus, Phœbus, here
  Beside thy gold-shod feet I shear
My boyhood's hair so fair, so long
My mother's joy, behold it there,
Gone from me like my nurse's song !
A man from hence, O let me wear
Thy dark leaves round my temples bare,
Give me the ivy crown to-day,
Place in my hand the bough of bay !

THE SPHYNX.

I.

'TIS said that Homer, blind and old,
  Wandered round the great lone Sphynx :
I see him blind and all alone,
Grope round that vast misshapen stone
  To discern the sense untold,
The answer from our ear that shrinks,
The mystery no hand can hold.

Did he discover even the shape—
Feel what the giant mass expressed—
Recognise the eyes agape—
Know what the monstrous claws confessed ?
Poet of poets, greatest one
Born of the Hellenic sun,
Who made the grand song still we sing,
Groping blindly and alone
Round that arcane misshapen stone ;
Did it tell thee anything ?

II.

THE poet old we still revere,
 Passed to sing of sword and spear.
In a long thereafter year,
The holy Child, as Scriptures say,
 Into Egypt fled away
To find repose a year and day :
 And in the night,
Beneath the saffron-hued moonlight,
Against the saffron-coloured sky,
The Sphynx stood their steps too to greet:
And Mary, with the Child divine,
Slept between its mighty feet,
Sheltered there as in a shrine ;
 Behold, the light
From out the Child, the Child divine,
Shone up into the vast wide eyes,
And made the arching eyelids bright
Against the darkening midnight skies.

NATURE.

FROM home did then the infant come
      When it came here?
Do we return unto that home
Beyond the day we disappear?
Then this fair Earth is but the place
      Where goal to goal
      We run a race,
And Nature, dame with sun-browned face,
Is but step-mother to the soul.

Step-mother, dear full-breasted queen!
When the true mother hides unseen,
The naked suckling to thy heart
Thou pressest: never would he part
Could he but remain, I ween!

II.

ON a rock limpet-crusted, one still day
    We sat ; the sun upon the white sea shone ;
Ripples like living arrows came right on
From rock to rock ; a mist harmoniously
United earth and heaven in silvery-grey.
    I said, there's nought to wish for more ; but she,
    The loved one, my companion, smiled at me ;
Yet she too by the charm was borne away.

Alas, this charm was broken by my deed ;—
    I strike the limpets off to see them fall,
And by strange instinct drawn from far, crabs speed
Along the water floor, crabs all astir,
    To tear the limpets from their shells ! A pall
Was lowered 'tween Nature and our faith in her.

I.

' FEEBLE waifs on darkling strand;
    Lost the power of heart or hand;
Better the vilest starveling slave,
In daylight other side the grave ;
Would that I, like thee, could go !'
So said the king of Grecian men
    To his questioner below.
But a mightier teacher rose
Over Calvary's empty tomb,
    And haply then
That future country lost its gloom ;
More lovely in that world than this,
Immaculate the white lily grows,
And perfected we walk in bliss.

II.

'WHEN blooms are best, they 'gin to go !'
    Our moralising gardener said ;
Yes, it must indeed be so,
Thus nature's cycle must be read.

But if the longing of the heart
Is to be listened to at all,
'Tis merely sad from friends to part,
When the face turns against the wall.

The curtain falls this side the sun,
But we upon the farther side
Shall find another walk begun
With flowers as fair on fields as wide.

If this hath been so from of old,
What multitudes of souls wake there !
Their earth-like motives dead and cold,
With other names, if names they bear.

Thus we grope this side the sun,
Blind-folded children play just so :
Time is eternity begun,
' When blooms are best, they 'gin to go.'

III.

MICHAEL ANGELO.

PERHAPS,—the future still must be
  The great Perhaps,—love still will reign
Beyond the dark unsounded sea,
Sympathy be our guide again.

Perhaps some difference will remain
Between the weaker and the strong,
So we may recognise, regain,
The greater chiefs of art and song.

Perhaps a single one at least
Of all the race !   If this is so,
Then we shall know our great high-priest,
Our strongest, Michael Angelo.

WHEN Columba brought his band
From old Erin's Christian land
To Iona's rock-bound strand,
He brought for each a sack of corn
And a grinding-stone, as well
As book and bell.
Then every morn
Each one alternate, great or small,
From the saint to little Saul,
Ground the daily meal for all :
For Christ said once in Galilee,
The greatest shall the servant be.
Now when it came the master's turn,
Little Saul's kind heart did burn
To see him shut his book and go
Alone into that granarie ;
Alone, but lo
Once in, an angel shut the door,
And set him down the quern before,

Saying, ' My father, I am here
    Even as a son,
To do for thee as thou hast done
For the heathen dark and poor,
Whereby ye gave our Lord good cheer.
I am strong, but thou art great,
So thus at thy right hand I wait,
    And here I be,
To grind this morning's meal for thee,
If thou wilt read the morning's psalm,
    I too may need the balm.'

These words the brethren heard below,
The quern then with great force did go,
And the saint began also
To read the psalter sweetly slow :
    Jesu pie auctor lucis
    Sis dux nobis viâ crucis.
Crowding around the planken door,
Through hinge and seam, upon the floor
They saw the angel : wing and hair,
And the garment that he wore,
Were all one colour they declare,

Yellow as flowers the sea-flags bear.
  Supplicantem audi chorum,
  O rex Jesu angelorum.
In joyful silence, one and all
Upon their knees these brethren fall,
Till ceased the noisy grinding-stone,
And lo ! Columba was alone.

OF ME.

OUR grandsire poets often prayed
   All the nine muses for their aid !
But I, who only wander round
      Familiar ground,
By pleasant autumn hedges bound,—
      Sure I can pray
For inspiration much more near ;
      My audience dear,
Assist me to a theme to-day !

You cannot help me ? but I see
I have a readier prompter here,
The child is whispering in my ear,
' Write a pretty thing of me !'
I will, you egotistic gnome,
The best is often nearest home.

LITTLE BOY.

I.

LITTLE boy, whose great round eye
    Hath the tincture of the sky,
Answer now, and tell me true,
Whence and what and why are you ?
And he answered, ' Mother's boy.'
        Yes, yes, I know,
        But 'twas not so
        Six years ago.
You are mother's anxious joy,
        Mother's pet,
        But yet—
A trouble came within the eye
That had some tincture of the sky.

II.

I LOOKED again, within that eye
    There was a question, not reply—
I only shaded back his hair,
    And kissed him there ;
    But from that day
There was more thinking and less play ;
    And that round eye,
That had a tincture of the sky,
Was somewhat shaded in its sheen ;
It looked and listened far away,
As if for what can not be seen.

III.

WHEN I turned about and cried,
　　But who am I
Prompting thus the dawning soul ?
　　I cannot hide
　　The want of a reply,
Though travelling nearer to the goal
Where we take no note of time :
I can only say I AM,
A phrase, a word, that hath no rhyme,
The name God called Himself, the best
To answer the weak patriarch's quest.

IV.

WHY talk nonsense to a child?'
　　Asks the mother from the fire,
Listening through both back and ears,
Listening with a mother's fears':—
　Already is he something wild,
Says that he can fly down stair !
　　　I do desire
You questioning men would have a care,—
He is my child, my only one,
You'll make him try to touch the sun !'

BAGATELLE.

I PLAY so false, my hand and sight
  Are both at fault: you win of right;
Let's change the scene; so deep, so clear,
The sky is, yet few stars appear;
And one black field the whole earth lies;
I must confess that great moon's light
Took me with a keen surprise.

Thou Moon, because thou art so white,
We call thee patient, pure, and wise,
Alone too in this vast wide night,
Blue-black the colour of death's fold,—
We call thee goddess: unshared might
Is thine, supreme, without emprise,
Above all taint of wrong or right!
While we in manifold disguise,
Shut within this lamplit hold,
Play trivial games in time's despite,
To make life shorter and less cold.

MARE SERENITATIS.

THERE is a void mysterious space
  Upon the full moon's face
They call Serenity's dead sea ;
Changeless and blank it seems to be
Amidst continuous change elsewhere,
Untouched by tides or waves of air,
Volcanic craters yawning round.

What breathless monsters harbour there,
If any life at all may dare,
Their iron lungs in silence bound,
Silence for ever and profound !

The little boy with thinking eyes,
Steals inquiringly to me :—
Tell you more of that moon-sea
I pointed out in last night's skies ?
But more no man can ever know,
We must not think of it at all,—
For if by sympathy I go
Too near that breathless sea, dear elf,
'Tis very likely I shall fall
Into breathlessness myself.

A GENIUS?

(w. a. c. s.)

IN early morn he rose elate,
　　Rose up with the strength of ten,
We recognised a king of men.
He would not linger, could not wait,
Opened at once the golden gate
And entered to the unlit shrine,
Poured out, yea, drank, the lustral wine.

But soon he found daylight more fair
Than the closed sanctum's darkened air ;
That the world outside was wide ;
That in all time there is a tide ;
That it is best to serve the call
To do what's waited for by all ;
That it is something less than sane
What has been done to do again.
Back he turned without a sigh,
And threw his magic passport by.
He said, ' I am not asked for there,
My harvest grows, it seems, elsewhere,
Upon another hemisphere.'
I wait him still, but wait in vain,
I shall not see his face again.

THE TWO SIDES.

LIFE is a fardel filled with care—
 Life is beautiful everywhere—
Life is, alas, a compromise—
Life is boundless like the skies—
Life goes with music to each part—
 All minor notes that wound the heart—
At life's feast Hebe's self appears—
 Life is God's chalice filled with tears.

Yes, yes, ye both are right, pardie!
 It well may be,
The gorgeous gold of sunset's glare
Is mid-day grey and cold elsewhere.

SELF-ACCUSATION.

' I SHALL not think of it again,'
　　He said, but took with him the pain
Starting for a distant goal :
Years after, in another land,
　　He took my hand,
And said, ' I think of that deed still,
Though on this further side the hill.'
I made this image of his soul.

Along a wave-lashed darkling strand
I saw a naked creature run,
And like himself another one,
Alike in shape, alike in size,
But darker and with fierier eyes,
Ran with him just one step behind,
With equal speed against the wind,
Filling his footprints on the sand
Of that restless ever-sounding sea :
And there, alas, they still may be.

THE SUN-DIAL.

L ET us read this ancient thing,
    The bronze plate on our dial stone :
Here's Father Time upon the wing.
His scythe too by which all is mown :
Here stars and zodiac signs profound
Are graven all the circle round :
A moralising motto too
In Latin cut, but not quite new,
Completes the decorated ring.

How many golden days there are
In this our life-year's calendar !
Each one diverse is with some,
As with the traveller far from home ;

With others show they all one strain,
Like a child's white daisy-chain,
Or a book without a stain,
And sooth to say, without a dower.
By the shadow of the Past,
Upon the sun-smit dial cast,
We know the Present passing hour.
Why should the motto then be new,
To decorate this dial stone,
With that thin green moss overgrown ?
It is enough if it be true.

THE SUN-DIAL.

II.

AROUND this sun-dial daughter May
　　Sometimes holds a holiday;
She is the matron, makes the tea;
The kettle by the gnomon stands:
We think the scene right fair to see,
As all scenes are when love commands.

I am too old for such a sphere,
Yet comet-like I venture near,
And so, perhaps, I overhear
Their talk of books, or of the play
Our laureate made but yesterday,
In which the Terry speaks a prayer
To great Diana Hecate,
A prayer that makes the bridegroom fear
There's dangerous thunder in the air.

Then daughter May, I do declare,
Repeats comments I made myself,
Yet is not in the least aware
Each word was mine, the innocent elf!
A maiden soul whose heart is free
A crystal globe is, where we see
Prophetic visions flash and fly.
And here's the little boy too, he
Must make himself a pleasantry!
He almost blushes, feels too shy
To sit in that sweet company:
'I am the only gentleman,'
He said to nurse, and off he ran,
But soon we found him mounted near,
Where hid he could both see and hear:
Already, very strange indeed,
In his small heart is sown Love's seed!

MORALITY.

I.

THE watcher watching from within !
    To know him well, we scarce can win,
Because the eye looks out, not in.
Call him Soul or what you will,
This watcher watching from within,
From his involved and secret cell
Can oftentimes but faintly tell
What is the wrong and what the right,
What may be good, what may be ill,
Which is the sin and which the crime ;
Life moves between these, Ill and Good
Can interchange, well understood,
As angel Day and dæmon Night
Divide for us our earth-born time.

II.

BESIDES, 'twas God's progressive
  plan

Before we straightened up to Man,

The instincts ruled in place of mind :

And even now, although consigned

The late born reasoning soul to serve,

They obey the Sympathetic Nerve,—

Inherited anatomies still

Ordering our acts against our will.

IN the first watch of the night,
　　One candle all my light,
I saw a Spirit near the door
Standing raised above the floor,
In the air he was, yet standing,
Feet placed flat as on some landing ;
So I turned my elbowed chair.
　　He stood still there,—
Like tarnished silver, dark yet bright,
　　And edging his crisp hair,
His hands,—whatever parts were bare,
Except the soles of his firm feet,
Passed a line of phosphor light :
Then noiselessly I rose to greet
My visitor as it was meet ;
　　I had no fears ;
His lips moved not, yet answered he,
Nor did I hear him through the ears ;
　　Ah, would I could
Repeat again his speech to Thee !
It satisfied and strengthened me,
It was Æolian too, I heard,
But yet I think he spoke no word.

THE old witch-wife beside her door
　　Sat spinning with a watchful ear,
A horse's hoof upon the road
　　Is what she waits for, longs to hear.

The mottled gloaming dusky grew,
　　Or else we might a furrow trace,
Sowed with small bones and leaves of yew,
　　Across the road from place to place.

Hark he comes !　The young bridegroom,
　　Singing gaily down the hill,
Rides on, rides blindly to his doom,
　　His heart that witch hath sworn to kill.

Up to the fosse he rode so free,
　　There his steed stumbled and he fell,
He cannot pass, nor turn, nor flee ;
　　His song is done, he 's in the spell.

She dances round him where he stands,
　　Her distaff touches both his feet,
She blows upon his eyes and hands,
　　He has no power his fate to cheat.

' Ye cannot visit her to-night,
　Nor ever again,' the witch-wife cried ;
' But thou shalt do as I think right,
　And do it swift without a guide.

' Upon the top of Tintock hill
　This night there rests the yearly mist,
In silence go, your tongue keep still,
　And find for me the dead man's kist.

' Within the kist there is a cup,
　Thou 'lt find it by the dead man's shine,
Take it thus ! thus fold it up,—
　It holds for me the wisdom-wine.

' Go to the top of Tintock hill,
　Grope within that eerie mist,
Whatever happens, keep quite still
　Until ye find the dead man's kist.

' The kist will open, take the cup,
　Heed ye not the dead man's shine,
Take it thus, thus fold it up,
　Bring it to me and I am thine.'

He went, he could make answer none,
  He went, he found all as she said,
Before the dawn had well begun
  She had the cup from that strange bed.

Into the hut she fled at once,
  She drank the wine ;—forthwith, behold !
A radiant damozel advance
  From that black door in silken fold.

The little Circe flower she held
  Towards the boy with such a smile
Made his heart leap, he was compelled
  To take it gently as a child.

She turned, he followed, passed the door,
  Which closed behind : at noon next day,
  Ambling on his mule that way,
The Abbot found the steed, no more,
  The rest was lost in glamoury.

MORNING.

FAIR morn, whose promise never dies,
  Distributor of gifts, fair morn !
She seems to blow a magic horn,
From the conscious tops of hills,
That makes the world lift glad fresh eyes,
All the trees quiver, and the rills
Leap forward with a child's surprise :
   The spell of dreams
Fades before that magic voice,
Nature calling to rejoice,
Everything in earth or air,
   Answers everywhere,
Making rainbows span the skies,
Scattering flowers on hastening streams,
  Fulfilling prophecies.

SPEECH is silver, silence gold :

      Speech goes out,

      Speech roams about,

To market flies, is bought and sold :

Silence at home spins fold on fold,

      Folds thick or thin

      To wrap her in,

      Thoughts strong or weak,

Spins she round her body bare,

Having nothing else to wear :

But speech is silver, silence gold ! |

      Why should we speak ?

HOW would the centuries long
    asunder,
Look on their sires with angry wonder,
Could some strong necromantic power
Revive them for one spectral hour !
Bondsmen of the past are we,—
Predestined bondsmen : could we see
The dead now deified, again
Peering among environing men,
    We might be free !

ONCE a rose ever a rose, we say,
    One we loved and who loved us
Remains beloved though gone from day ;
To human hearts it must be thus,
The past is sweetly laid away.

Sere and sealed for a day and year,
    Smell them, dear Christina, pray ;
So nature treats its children dear,
So memory deals with yesterday,
The past is sweetly laid away.

PRAYERLESS from the sacred well,
From Castaly and Hippocrene,
He drank, and on the verge of hell
Slept, and forgot where he had been,
When he returned to common day,
Baptized by Hecate !

He was the aeronaut who flew
Through skies becoming black like night,
Above the wrack and mountain range :
Saw his own shadow on the white
Cloud-world below that dazed his sight,
And with his lapsing sense scarce knew
That moving phantom, phantom strange,
Was his own shadow. It was he
Who lay in fever frenziedly,
And chased the printed flowers that shed
A mad confusion round his bed,
Until at last they changed and past
Into vermin round the dead.

'GO,' said the Cardinal Bellay,
    'See how my doctor fares to-day.'
The page skipped off from house to house,
But entered like a noiseless mouse,
Hearing the priest read near the bed,
Where the patient lay as dead;
So just within the door he said—
'My lord the Cardinal Bellay
Asks how the doctor fares to-day?'

The young voice touched the wandering head:
'Say he's about to take the leap:
Within the dark—
        About to sleep,—
Would that be better?—

He must go
To solve the great Perhaps, just so—
Tell him that '—

'Dear brother, nay,'
The good priest rising up did say,
'Beati qui in *Domino*
Moriuntur !'—

'Well then, stay,'
Muttered the dear old Rabelais ;
'Bring it me at once, my friend,
I never would the church offend,
It hangs upon that peg you know,
By all means bring my *domino*.'

I.

LIKE wayward flocks of lambs and sheep,
    We Clouds upon the soft warm sky,
Over hamlet, vale, or steep,
Gather or scatter, faint or fly,
White and bright from land to land,
From hill to hill, by light winds fanned :
As travellers loitering on their track,
Or bather slumbering on his back,
Children of the sun-god are we
O'er harvest champaign, teeming sea ;
In this the noontide of our day
We laugh at change, yet must not stay.

II.

OH blood-red change ! all passed away,
   All passed with him the lord of Life :
We, hid in blank night, well-a-day !
Powerless, lost to joys or strife,
Lost to ourselves, lost, lost are we,
By soulless winds on soulless sea,
Swathed, blindfolded, rolled along
Beyond man's voice or angel's song,
Unseen e'en by cold stars we hie
Far up within black wastes of sky,
Wrapped in shrouds of darkest spun,
Never more to see the sun.

OF POETRY.

I.

THE POET.

THE poet has been called of old,
　　Maker, seeker, finder, singer :
Which of these names, I would be told,
Best describes our best joy bringer.

　Maker?　not more than he or she
Who makes your gloves or makes my tea.
　Seeker?　yes, too oft I fear,
So call not him we hold so dear.
　Singer?　never is he set
To music but it makes him fret.
　Finder?　yes, he finds the word
We leap to meet whenever heard,
The best of living words, that linger
In the warmth about the heart,
Warm it comes beneath his finger,
　Never more with it we part.

II.

THE POET'S BOOK.

THE harmonies the poet knows
    Are like the petals of this rose,
Leaf over leaf so pure, so bright,
So perfumed in crimson light,
Another still, they still combine,
Like verse on verse and line on line.

Silent he hides within his book,
Like hermit wise in sainted nook,
A sheath'd sword, unseen bird in bower—
The nightingale in night's high tower,
A voice not wandering but held close
Within the petals of his Rose.

III.

ART FOR ART'S SAKE.

'ART for art's sake,'—very well,
　　Your picture you don't care to sell?
Yes, yes, I do, and thus I try
To paint so bright they want to buy--
'Art for art's sake,'—then I fear
You want no sympathetic tear
From the stalls and boxes here?
Yes, yes, I do, I write it so,
A hundred nights the crowds shall go—
'Art for art's sake,'—Heavens ! once more,
You'd say again things said before?
And pray, why not? I wish I could
Stand as Shakespeare, Fletcher, stood—
Nay, dear aspirant, rather write
As Shakespeare were he here to-night;
That would be far more worth prizing :—
But who can rise to that high pass—
　　Who can *rise?* alas, alas,
Shakespeare little thought of rising !

IV.

ANCIENT FORMS.

SUCH, valued friend, you tell me these
   Old forms, like pictures Japanese,
Are neat and curious, justly please ;
Difficult also.   Without doubt
To dance in chains, or spite of gout,
Is difficult, painful too ; but that
Is weak ; the thought is speech's law
    And poet's bond ;
He's no mere verbal acrobat.

Should every flower have but one frond,
Two blooms, three seeds, without a flaw ?
The poet has some sweet thing to cry—
Well, let him speak straight from the heart,
And so its fairest shades impart
    Harmoniously :
Spontaneous speech sets faith at ease :

But full-grown men now take small part
In our linguistic filagrees,
Our squeezing truth into a mould,
That may but inexactly hold.
You think so too, yet tell me still
These verses unforeseen, at will
Running like a running rill,—
Verses free as if they grew,
For ears refined will scarcely do.

That is a pity, dilettanti
Sometimes of brains, not ears, are scanty ;
An amateur once said to me,
' Frame makes the picture, do you see ! '
I smiled and could not quite agree—
' But you're the painter ! answered he ;
So I'm the poet, born or made,
And were I not the least afraid,
To show my great hope quite unfurled,
I'd say we write for all the world.

Oh, if you go so fast, so high,
Sweeping the cobwebs from the sky,
I shall no further make reply.

V.

ON READING MR. THEODORE WATTS' SONNET,

'THE SONNET'S VOICE.'

AN art grows up from year to year :
 The critic weighs the utmost gains,
The last result, the perfect sphere,
Not the steps, but what remains ;

Sees the analogue, ebb and flow,—
Beautiful, yes, look at it near,—
The flow, the ebb returning so,—
It is at last art's perfect sphere.

But not the less our Shakespeare knew
Another way ; by full discourse
To show his picture as it grew,
Worked out in many-sided force.

 Then when the heart can wish no more,
 With a strong couplet bars the door.

VI.

REMONSTRANCE.

(ON SOME POEMS NOW WITHDRAWN).

O F all my favourite leaves these three
　　Appear to me
The wisest in their own degree,—
But my good arbitress would hear
　　No more, she stopt her ear,
And said, 'That surely cannot be,
They are so sad, so hard to see,—
Philosophy is not poesy.'

No, not oftentimes, alas,
And yet the obverse ought to hold,
Ere the poet can be crowned with gold :
At least for once, pray, let them pass,

Indeed you ought,
They cost their maker so much thought :
Perhaps the lines are wingèd seeds !

' Perhaps they are, but then of weeds ! '

Of weeds ? then weeds medicinal.

' But still would I their flight recall,
Physic is only for our needs !
Let us to the garden go,
In the garden roses grow.'

OF POETS.

I.

STRATFORD.

THIS is the street where Shakespeare's
  childhood grew
To Shakespeare's manhood, back to which
  he drew,
To walk in peace along the paths he knew.
At morn and eve of quiet days
To hear the small birds' well-known lays,
To see the bat flit noiselessly,
And rooks against the molten sky,
He passed the loud-mouthed audience by,
And left to all the winds of fate
The poet's immortality,
Yea, even to the green-room care
Heminge and Condell had to spare.
So act the strong self-centred great !
' Children we are as ye,' they say,
' Players, spectators, for life's day,
  Which are the masters of the play ?'

II.

SHAKESPEARE.

GIVE me but fame ! the poetaster cries,
    Standing on tiptoe so to touch the skies.

Why gather empty shells by God's ebb-shore,
    Vital no more,
Records of what has been, what matter they ?
My soul's in mine own hand to-day ;—
Quoth Shakespeare, and to Stratford bent his
    way.

III.

THE KESSELSTADT MASK.

(FROM AN ARTISTIC POINT OF VIEW).

THAT round-cheeked, flat-faced Stratford bust
　　Sank one's ideal to the dust,
But heaven be praised, for by its grace
We have found our Shakespeare's face.

Gerard's own bust they well could spare,
So they mounted it up there !
As for the portrait by Droeshout,
Perhaps his fingers had the gout !

But here's the king of men divine,—
The Elizabethan profile line,—
Let Gerard and Droeshout give place—
We have found our Shakespeare's face.

IV.

DANTE. I.

BEFORE the dawn of modern day,
    Saint Francis and Saint Dominic
Forgathered on sweet Fiesole.
They waled from all the young and quick
The tenderest heart on all the earth,
Now, said they, this thin heart and we
Shall make a bond, and it shall be
'Tween poetry and sulphurous fear;
Nor any more shall love make mirth
In Italy our garden dear,
Nor manhood's virtues hold a part
In our Italian rhythmic art.

So then, from market or from well,
The women ran when Dante passed,
The cruel sight-seer back from Hell
Had borne with him an evil blast;
And though from Paradise at last
He brought some flowers of asphodel,
The compact hath not passed away
Made then upon sweet Fiesole.

V.

DANTE. II.

A CELTIC saint the tale once told,—
   Ere Dante's birth the tale was old—
That he in faith, with mortal eyes
Had been uplifted through the skies,
And saw the winged in Paradise.
He had been hand led down below
Where Purgatorial sulphurs flow,
And round the furthest confines there
Had seen the vast high wall of H ell :
But not even angel-guides could tell
What horrors Satan might prepare
For inmates at the Judgment-knell ;
As yet it was a waste, no soul
Till then might reach that hopeless goal.
But Dante forestalled time, full well
He knew the pits and filled all Hell.

VI.

DANTE AND BEATRICE.

A H, did she pass so coldly by
      The tenderest love in all the earth,
Making his lifetime one long sigh,
That never knew a morn of mirth?
High up the Paradisal stair
Did he refind amidst the glare
This matron's breast without a heart,
Transformed to Theologic Art?

Ah, well for us 'tis not our part
In England's fresher, stronger air,
To shrine this saint-elected pair,
This mythologic, cleric dream,
Instead of Shakespeare, our supreme,
Humane, and multiform, and clear,
Exhaustless, blood-red, near and dear.

VII.

WORDSWORTH.

EARTH ! through whom we come and go,
  Mother of Prometheus ! fair
Thy temples rose in warmer air,
Thou many-breasted, ever young,
To sounding cymbals wast thou sung
    Two thousand years ago ;
      Yet here again
The wisest man of many men,
The truest bard of latest days
Has made his life thy hymn of praise.

VIII.

SOUTHEY.

ON READING 'THE LIFE,' BY PROFESSOR DOWDEN.

JOB heard a sweet sound, Job awoke,
  And saw a faint white light,
He turned, he deemed the night was spent,
'Twas but the first watch of the night,
  Day had not broke,
It was Jehovah's angel spoke,
Bright in the opening of the tent.

Job, the Lord hath heard your prayer,
And sends me here to thee, I bear
Your recompense, which shall it be,
Goodness or Greatness? say and see.

Job knelt, Lord, give me charity,
The rest perhaps will come to me.

He looked, the angel was no more,
Job rose in purple from the floor.

IX.

BURNS.

HIS COTTAGE AND MONUMENT.

THIS is the cottage as it was of old,
    The window four small panes, and in the
      wall
The box-bed where the first daylight did fall
Upon their new-born infant : narrow fold
And poor, when times were hard and winds were cold
    As they were still to him. And now close by
    Above Corinthian columns mounted high,
The famed Choragic Tripod shines in gold !

The lumbering carriages of these dull years
    Have pass'd away, their dust has ceased to whir
Round the pedestrian, silent to our ears
    Is that maelstrom of Scottish men, this son
    Of that poor cot we count the kingliest one ;
Such is time's justice, time the harvester.

X.

CHATTERTON.

OH cruel night, that closed those questioning
eyes,—

Nay, kindly say, stars shine in darkening skies.

Oh cruel night, that stopped those wondering ears,—

Nay, kindly say, who knows what now he hears?

XI.

SAPPHO.

S ISTERS ! sisters Nine and mine !

Take my latest lustral wine ;

This lyre no more to be attuned by me,

I dedicate,

Alas, too late,

Brass-hearted Artemis, to thee ;

And this, my weary body, to the sea.

XII.

ORPHEUS.

THY mother, Calliope, gave thee power
  Over the heart of man, above the laws
Of savage nature : in the perilous hour
Over the triple Dog's dismembering claws;
Ixion leant a moment on his wheel,
And Tantalus forgot his thirst to feel,
When thy voice throughout hell began to peal :
But not the Nine, nor even the Gods, can save
Their best-beloved children from the grave.

XIII.

BYRON.

H E was Childe Harold pacing there
The dark deck of that exile-ship,
When twenty years scarce fringed his lip,
Pacing in a boy's despair.

He was Don Juan, not too soon
Sent from the glimpses of the moon.

And had he lived a little longer,
He would have risen greater, stronger;
King of the Greeks, he had been then
Agamemnon, King of men.
Yet not the best of warriors he
Who crossed towards Troy the Ægean sea.

XIV.

SHELLEY. I.

THE three words yet to dominate
  This world with peace and love elate,
We rede upon the ruined wall Palatial,
Once the witless Bourbon's pride,
Words written large from side to side;
And on the pavement where we stood
      Lay fratricidal blood.
What wonder then eyes fixed so far,—
Faith and to-day so coiled in war,—
Directest steps may go amiss?
Inspiréd speech be vague as his?

Yet shall these three words be one day,
Our full-grown manhood's rondelay,
The sensitive plant shall surely grow
Beside the myrtle and the bay,
When we with him have passed away,
      And shall not know.

XV.

SHELLEY. II.

THAT reason-born millennium,
 He thought so near, shall surely come,
Shall come when days have longer grown,
 And nights are longer too,
When bread from richer tilth is mown,
And all our powers are born anew:
Millions of years far off, may be,
Eons of ages, it shall come,
But then the Poet men may see
Shall throw all our poetics dumb.
For then, as now, the poet's lyre
Must shine with light as well as fire;
And he sings best whose clear plain song
Beats with our hearts and makes us strong.

THAT leaf, the earliest of the year
  To fall, hath dropped upon your hair,
I saw it wavering in the air,
Then drop as if directed where !
Vain fancies ! it bodes nought to fear,
   Even let it lie ;—
Doubtless to you, to me, to all
   From out eternity,
Hours all foredoomed are hastening near,
Although they are not to be seen
   Against the sky,
Nor do we hear a doomster call !
Yet this first leaf to fall though green,
Upon your head, my daughter May,
   Hath fallen to-day !

LEFT ALONE.

I PACE the garden paths alone,
   Waiting till the close of day ;
It is not well aloud to moan,
So end I this small book straightway.
Silence goes with me gently here,
Within, it sits wrapped round with fear.
So, gloaming-lit I walk and pray
Now to be led in God's right way,
     And made to say
Even thus His will, not mine, be done,
Though not the less the mid-day sun
Has lost for me its light and heat ;
His will, and only His, is meet.

AUBADE.

THAT sycamore leaf! I knew it fell
    Upon my heart as well
As on the head of my dear May,
And I have brooded all the night
In fear I would be left alone
With all my thoughts as cold as stone,
    Fancying what words to say.
But with the blessed gift of light
The faint delusions passed away,
I raised the casement to the thrill
Of morn, a bird upon the sill
Alit and sang a song so gay,
Its echo follows, follows still :
So all night's phantoms fly with day.

WEAR thou this fresh green garland this one
      day,
This white-flowered garland wear for Love's delight,
While still the sun shines, ere the lessening light
Declines into the shadows cold and grey :
Wear thou this myrtle leaf while yet ye may,
    Love's wings are wings that hate the dews of night,
    Nor will he rest still smiling in our sight,
And still companioning our western way.

Wear then this plain green garland this one day,
    To please Love's eyes, else not for all the might
    Of all the gods, nor any law of right,
Will he, content with age's disarray,
For us pass by the youthful and the gay ;
    And it were hard to live in love's despite.

DINNER and day together go,
　　As round the table still we dwell,
Watching the sun descending slow,
Our faces shine with day's farewell.

This is the moment of all time
When stillness reigneth over all :
When life calms down, the highest lime
Moves not, nor any leaf dares fall.

Shall we sit still in low-voiced talk
Anticipating lamp and book,
Or once more take a sauntering walk
Hill-ward to catch the sun's last look ?

The lambs and sheep have parted long,
No anxious bleat nor moor-hen's call
Is heard, nor robin's autumn song,
Absolute stillness reigns o'er all.

Over the orange-tinted brae,
Against that wondrous north-west sky,
Over the far sea golden-gray,
Where no horizon we descry.

AN AUTUMN EVENING.

A glorified world is there, behold,
Above that cloud-bank growing dim,
Where the great king hath laid his head,
Fragments of crimson still unfold :
Cherubim's wings are ruby red,
So these may be the cherubim !

Now we return with noiseless tread,
These cottage doors are shut betimes,
Listen, this is old John Grimes',
He reads before he goes to bed ;

He reads a chapter of the Book
Of Books, to comfort his old wife,
Happily in this far Scotch nook,
Faith still trims the lamp of life.

But there our own high windows shine,
The evening fire is lit we see,
Wayfaring shoes let us resign,
And you will sing that hymn to me.

THEY're in the corner of the field,
　　The last field they shall have to shear,
They've left and tied one bunch, 'the hare,'
Called in harvest language here.
So I shall leave my books and toys,
　　My Nankin blues and other pets,
For still to pass on pleasantly
　　One must pay dame fashion's debts.

To give the prize, the silver coin,
　　To him who hits the mark, or she,
I hope indeed it may be Jane,
　　Who makes the sickle rightly flee,
To cut the bunch, to kill 'the hare,'
　　The last grain cut of all the year :
But no, it is douce Donald Bain,
　　So rarely fate accords a cheer !

Already the wide kitchen blooms
   With wreaths of evergreens and flowers,
The solid roasts are almost done,
   To try their gathered festive powers.
All disappear till evensong,
   And then we see the fiddle-case,
With gay escort of twos and threes,
   Girls and their lovers drest with grace.

The hour arrives, the ample board
   Is girt by young and old alike,
Anon it disappears, and then
   Twenty pairs of hands they strike,
The fiddler mounts, the dance begins,
   Now Jane could win the prize, I think,
Scotch reel, mazurka, quadrille, waltz,
She make's old Fergie's eyelids wink.

The Drennens too, good sonsy pair,
   Passed their silver wedding day,

Admired by their own children too,
  Dance with each other, dance alway.
Now you and I, old Fergie, come,
  We elders may still try, you know,
No, no ! take Mysie, I've no breath,
  That indeed would make me crow !

Too soon the tall house-clock strikes twelve,
  The lads and lasses hear it too,
I leave them to their parting reel,
  And write this plain song, friend, for you.

MEMORY.

Last night I lost a word, the one
  Just wanted for my madrigal :
Then went to bed disconsolate,
Groping through a web half spun,
Listening for sounds beyond recall :
Unrhymed my ruined verses hung,
Till I was lost myself—had won
Within the silence-hingéd gate,
      The gate of horn :
      And lo, at morn
I found the word upon my tongue.

It was so in my school-boy year,
   When the lesson would not lie
   Within the jaded memory,
   With day-light it would reappear,
      Unravelled, clear.

MEMORY.

Perhaps 'twill be so that dread morn
　　Far beyond the gate of horn ;
　All we have said, or thought, or done,
　Like blades in a grass-field in the sun,
　　Innumerable and clear each one,
　Will present be, no loss and no decay
Of all our growth throughout life's play :—
　　And that will be our Judgment day :
　　Ourselves the judge, the judged, the soul
　　To be advanced, from goal to goal !

A ND yet I am as one who looks behind,
  A traveller in a shadowed land astray,
Passing and lost upon the boundary
Of actual things, who turns against the wind,
An hundred simulacral ghosts to find
    Close following, an hundred pairs of eyes
    Shining around like phosphorescent flies,—
And all of them himself, yet changed in kind.

Those once I was, which of them now am I ?
    Not one, all alien, long-abandoned masks,
    That in some witches' sabbath, long since past,
Did dance awhile in my life's panoply,
    And drank with me from out of the same flasks ;
    Am I not rid of these, not even at last ?

NAY, let me own it is but vain regret,
    Not wise, to disavow life's unity,
To cry out, Oh, it was a child, not I,
It was a boy, it was a lover's fret
Caught in the magic of a golden net,
    It was a run-away tracked by a hound
    He needs must slay, must tread into the ground,—
Groping about to find some oubliette.

It was the very self, the self indeed,
    Said the true word or thought the treacherous
        thought ;
The very self fate-driven, did the deed
    That won the prize, or black-crowned doomster
        brought :
And thus it is we look beyond the shore
That girds our isle, while Hope flies on before.

STEADILY burning like a lamp enshrined,
 The Sanscrit says our lives should pass
   away ;
Even so, but how to guard by night and day
This priceless lamp ? From the Unknown God's
 wind
Fans it for ever, joys and cares combined,
 The plague of fire and hail, in through the bars
 Of this our prison-house make constant jars ;
No heart of flesh can hold their powers confined.

Not then for us in Western lands is it,
 Where every hour brings loads enough for years,
Naked on contemplation's mat to sit ;
But woe to him who finds no time at all
For questioning, who sleeps in a festive hall ;
 Who finds no gains in long-remembered tears.

AGE.

'STEPPING westward,' did she say,
    At sunset on that long Scotch day?
'Stepping westward,' yes, alway,
With staff and scrip,
Wayfaring songs upon my lip,
Stepping, stepping, to the end.

As down the slanting path I wend,
Behold, a breadth of distant sea,
Between the hills on either hand,
Ships bearing from some unknown land
To other land unknown to me.

'Stepping westward,' all that be,
Body and soul, by land or sea,
Follow still the westering sun ;
That must end which has begun.

So many years I've gone this way,
  So many years ! I must confess
Waste energies, much disarray,
Yet can I own no weariness,
Nor see I evening's shadows fall
Down my much inscriptioned wall :
The warm air still is like mid-day,
And many mournful ghosts are past,
  Laid still at last.
The fabled fardel lighter grew
As near the bourne the bearer drew :
Life can, alas, no more surprise
By its continuous compromise.
New faces fill the chairs, and so
Our interest in the game runs low.
Quiet pleasures longest stay,
Experience packs so much away.

I wait and wonder : long ago
This wonder was my constant guest,
Wonder at our environing,
And at myself within the ring :
Still that abides with me, some quest
Before my footsteps seems to lie,
But quest of what I scarcely know,
Life itself makes no reply:
A quest for nought that earth supplies,
This is our life's last compromise.

So many years I've gone this way,
It seems I may walk on for aye,
' Long life God's gift,' a brother prayed,
Nearing the confines of the dead,
Going reluctant, not afraid :
With bated breath I bow the head
Thinking of those vague words to-day.

The ancient tempter well divined
This longing of the sunlit blind,

'Ye shall be wise as gods,' he said,
If ye obey me undismayed.
Ah, never may this be, though still
In hope we climb the topless hill.
'Tis but the ending of the strife
Calms and crowns the weary head,
Nor till the morn beyond our life
Can life's oracle be read,
When the unanswered brain and heart
Have ceased to ask and ceased to smart:
And all the centuries to come
Like centuries past to us be dumb.

A-DIEU.

FAREWELL, it is not much to say
    When bright night follows pleasant day,
And when the traveller takes the way
From friendly hearth to hearth of friend,
But yet with each change we portend
Some grief, some hand-long cloud of care
We ought to shelter from or share:
Parting eyes are over-kind,
The lamb-lost ewe's bleat fills the air,
The plover's plaint is in the wind.

EPILOGUE.

HERE then I draw my linked rein;
These months have filled the farmer's wain,
Filled too my small portfolio,
I need not wait the threatening snow:
Already on the steep Goatfell
Forebodingly we mark it well,
And leafless is the garden Bower,
Shed is every gentle flower.

The swallows have gone south, we too
Will go, and to these verses new
I add some old ones, one or two.
'Tis said what's new is seldom true,
And what is true can scarce be new.
I hope indeed it is not so,
But year by year fresh flowers shall blow,
For poets still to bring to you.

NOTES.

P. 14, '*School Children.*' Except very minor changes, necessary to accommodate the Rhymes sung by the children to the rest of the poem, they are here exactly given as sung by little girls in play in Ayrshire.

P. 25, '*Oisin.*' This legendary account of the end of the Irish Ossian, is derived from the ancient story of considerable length given in Dr. Joyce's very interesting 'Old Celtic Romances.'

P. 57, '*A Birthday.*' The rhyme shrieked out rather than sung by Scotch children at All Hallow tide, as the author has heard it, is this :—

> Heigh, how ! for Halloween,
> A' the fairies can be seen,
> Some blue and some green,
> Or freckled like a Turkey bean !

Mr. R. Chambers, however, gives it—

> Some black and some green,

adding that the black ones are the evil fairies, but the green are the 'Good People.' But are there any evil fairies, or are they only evil when badly treated ?

P. 60, '*Elijah.*' This was written after seeing Sir F. Leighton's noble picture in the Academy Exhibition.

P. 61, '*Love and Death*,' the reader will readily

see, has been suggested by G. F. Watts's painting of the same name.

P. 66, '*The Sphynx*, 11.' The description of the Virgin and Child sleeping between the paws of the statue is derived from a picture by M. Olivier Mersson, now in the large gallery built and filled with works of the French school by Mr. Duncan of Benmore, near Kilmun, on the Clyde.

P. 84, '*Self-accusation.*' The impressive symbol of the conscience following the accused like his Double, is from a drawing by my late brother David Scott.

P. 92, '*A Lowland Witch Ballad*' is founded on a rhyme still to be heard in the neighbourhood of Tintock hill. It is given as follows in Chambers's 'Popular Rhymes:'—

> On Tintock tap there is a mist,
> And in the mist there is a kist,
> In this kist there is a cap,
> And in the cap there is a drap.
> Take up the cap, drink aff the drap,
> And set it again on Tintock tap.

The small flowering weed, the Circe, or Magician's Nightshade, also introduced in the ballad, has the power attributed to it of making any one accepting it as a gift in love with the giver.

P. 112. The theory of the English form of the sonnet, as indicated here, has, I see, been expressed more at length by Mr. T. Hall Caine in the preface to his 'Three Centuries of Sonnets.' Mr. Theo. Watts's admirable sonnet, 'The Sonnet Voice,' which first appeared in the *Athenæum* 17th September 1881, is republished in that work.

NOTES.

117, '*Stratford.*' Perhaps the last lines of this poem may remind some readers of Shakespeare's reputed reply to Ben Jonson :—

JONSON.

If but stage-actors all the world displays,
Where shall be found spectators of the plays?

SHAKESPEARE.

Little or much of what we see we do,
We are all actors and spectators too.

An Aftermath.

INDEX.

INTRODUCTORY SONNET.

" GIVE me a pen, I will not hold you long,
  But I have some few words that I would say
Before I mount, before I pass away,
Following my friends all gone ; it is not wrong
What I would write, nor any foolish song,
  But now I stand beside the shoreless sea,
  A word or two from out my heart would flee
Not said before, that coming death makes strong."

How many have felt thus besides the brave
  Fair queen of womankind, the good Roland :
Life's long years past, both joyous years and grave
  The wish descends upon the untired hand
To leave some self-drawn picture, or some stave
  Of speech for those left waiting on the strand.

NEW YEAR BELLS.

TWO EPOCHS. I. 1831.

L ONG years ago, when love was lord of me
   And all good gifts were in the impending year,
At this same hour I heard afar and near
These New Year bells flood heaven with melody:
I, home bound through the snow, as over sea
   Voices of dear friends hail the mariner
   Returning prosperous : till in their rear
Saint Paul's great voice made lesser voices flee.

What mattered then beneath those hopeful bells
   The homeward walk by weary fortune given,
   The obscure future whersoever driven,
In years to come; all lost in those sweet knells
   High overhead, like messages from heaven.

NEW YEAR BELLS.

RING out again, ye Bells of Battersea,
   Over the seaward Thames while I sit here
   Lamplit, with moistened eye and hungering ear,
Recalling thoughts of things once hoped to be—
Past now, forgotten almost; for to me
   Those wild harmonies in the waves of air,
   Changing yet still repeating, here or there,
Yet truly ordered, ring life's history.

And still I hear them lovingly, good bells,
   Across the rushing river in the wind,
Fainting or rising as the tempest swells;
   The river rushing like dark years behind
Chasing dark years gone by, and those sweet spells
   High overhead with memories intertwined.

E ARLY astir in this midsummer time
      In the Queen's close, sweet hour in this sweet
         clime,
   I stray at will to hear the throstle sing
   Among the trees that round her garden cling ;
I, Ronsard, in my youthood's joyous prime,
And by the Queen's desire, beneath the lime
She loves, to sing to her again the rhyme,
      The daintiest of all the rhymes I bring,
                     My rhyme of Love.
But yet despite this July's leafy time,
The Queen's praise, birds' songs, odourous rose and
   thyme,
      This heartache close to me, so close, will cling
      Because, forsooth, the blue-eyed Lize took wing
When I yestreen began my daintiest rhyme,
                     My rhyme of Love.

SPRING.

WELCOME, Spring, too long delayed,
    Kindest, most reluctant maid :
Sweetest of younger sisters, simplest one
Of the bare bosomed chorus of the year.
    Now last season's beech-tree leaf
    Hath fallen. The crocus sends her spear
    Up through the earth, a little span
    Each day increasing to a sheaf.
    The housewife sings the damsel's song,
    The old man whistles like the boy,
    Aches no more his limbs annoy,
    He steps out like a sower strong.
Sweetest of younger sisters, odourous tressed
Forcefully wooed by sharp-hoofed breezes, Spring !
    Thy advent knows each living thing
    Through the dense deep earth impressed
    With love's light touch of wondrous flame,
    That sense and soul revives the same.

Summer, with her proud silence and her haze
Of heat, her gracious shadows, and her maze

SPRING.

Of leaves and undergrowths and rills
Dropping asleep beneath the cloudless hills,
    Hath no such kindly wing
    As thou, bird-hatching Spring.
Autumn, with her boisterous mirth
Shaking the red-ripe fruit upon the earth,
Shedding the rose leaves, each eve shedding too
From saddening clouds and stars great drops of dew,
    Hath not the prophet tongue,
    Like thine, thou ever young,
    Young as a child, thou bride more fair,
    Innocent as a blush, and strong
    As a lion in a poet's song.

May I then venture near thee, in thy hair
To place this pink-edged daisy, Sweet ?
    Alas, 'tis mortal even there,
    Mortal but saintly Margarite.
    The heedless sheep goes browsing on,
    The daisy from the grass is gone.
    Matron Summer is coming anear,
    To crown the still inconstant year :

SPRING.

But ere thou flyest, blue-eyed Spring,
    It suits us well to bring,
Bound by this withy of poetry,
An offering of thine own flowers to thee.

WM. BLAKE'S DESIGNS FOR THE GRAVE.

THERE was a time before the chick could fly,
    But still was screened by the maternal wing,
    He worshipped these as if they held a spring
Of living waters. Had not God on high
Shown innocent William what it was to die,
      Made him to know the rapture of the pain,
      When soul and body part to meet again :
Dread truths concealed within futurity.

And now that years have shriven and tortured me,
      When labouring much in thriftless fields hath
        filled
The tablets of my memory, these burn
With their old fires, within them still I see
      A hand inspired, though in his Art unskilled ;
My heart leaps up, my childhood's awes return.

ROME. TIME OF THE DESTRUCTION OF JERUSALEM.

THEN face to face the New Faith and the Old,
   The new Faith promising endless reign
Beyond the catacombs and martyr's pain ;
The mystic doctrines sacraments enfold
The scorn of learning, the contempt of gold.
      The Old Faith, fancy's foundling, faith of heart,
      Lighting small lamps to Lares, by the art
Of potter or of sculptor bought and sold.

This is the day of Triumph: lo, this hour
      Titus the conqueror enters, raised on high
The sacredest of Trophies borne to-day
By brutal soldiers, from them gone the power :
      Yet over all the wide world goes the cry,
Awake ! ye blind, arise, go hence away!

INFANCY.

"LET him lie still," the young wife cried, "right
    soon
    I shall be back," and on my lap she laid
    Her swaddled nurseling ; startled even dismayed,
I looked down on the face like a white moon,
On the closed eyes and open mouth, no spoon
    Had yet touched, and could see its breathing made
    The folds expand in which it was arrayed :
It was alive, yet knew not night from noon.

Beautiful was it ?   I can scarcely say.
    I never held so young a thing before ;
But wonderful it was to me, and may
    Be likened to a shrine within closed door,
Closed, unlit, but from whence a breath made way
    Te Deum laudamus, saying o'er and o'er.

AN ANNIVERSARY: THE 31st.

ADDRESSED TO A DEAR FRIEND.

SPRING comes with all the firstlings of the year
    Leaping around her, careless of the cold ;
  Soon summer's tale so charming will be told,
The last rose fall, the sun shrink as in fear ;
Alas, the weeks fly faster, and more near
    Yule seems to Easter, when the hair grows gray,
    Sooner it seems the swallows fly away,
And wintry floes brim full the shivering weir.

What matters it, these are old ills we know
    That pass us by as Chronos gives command :
But still your smile is bright as long ago,
Still can we gather shells on life's lee shore,
    We still can walk like children hand in hand,
Friendship and love beside us as of yore.

IN life we judge and estimate,
    With our dearest even debate,
And strive to hold the balance true
Between the brown eyes and the blue.
But with the dead we do not so ;
Shrined in the past we let them go
Their mystic journey high and far,
Until they pass the starlit bar
Dividing gods from things below:
And thus at last on chancel stones
We worship before empty thrones.

Could we wind back the skean of time
Ere Giotto's tower could bellman climb,
We might see Gemma, weary wife,
Nursing her babes in threadbare quoif—
One, two, three, four—alas they're seven,
Left to the charities of heaven !
We might see Dante, foiled in strife,
Thankless over strangers' bread,
Raking hell's fires on the dead;

Casting back on Florence fair
His bloodshot eyes, a hateful stare.
Not wise in guile or strong of arm,
To shield himself from bale or harm;
With powerless hate and childish lies
Inventing undreamt cruelties.

THE INFERNO.

A CELTIC Saint this tale first told,
    Ere Dante's birth the saint was cold,
But he in faith with mortal eyes
Had been uplifted through the skies
And seen the winged in Paradise.

Then was he hand-led down the stair
Where Purgatorial sulphurs flare,
And round the furthest confines there
Had seen the copeless walls of Hell,
But not even angel-guides could tell
What horrors Satan might prepare
For sinners at the Judgment knell.
At that time 'twas a waste, no soul
Till the last day could reach that goal !

But Dante forestalled time, too well
He loved the pits, and loved the spell
Of friends and foes foredoomed to hell.
Alas ! must we, at this late time,
Make our good God act Satan's part,

Accepting that accursed rhyme,
Forgiving blasphemy for art?
Is our paternal God displayed
In these vile cruelties arrayed?
Or is the poet before heaven,
Guilty of that sin ne'er forgiven?

RAPHAEL'S MADONNA DI SAN SISTO.

ONCE and once only, and no more,
   Art hath reached the topmost bough;
The goodliest fruit of all his store
Our well-filled garner holds till now.

Lo ! from a life-filled atmosphere
She comes with silent step with mild
And plaintive eyes bent sadly here
Holding her prize of prizes, her man-child,
King of the world-expected year,
Safe within her queenly arms
            Above all harms.

Once and once only, and no more,
Out of the sensuous classic night,
Born of the dusk mid-christian lore,
Into our midday's questioning light :
Behold ! Ideal womanhood,
Maternity, supremely good,
Self sacrificing, without stain ;
Goddess eternally serene,
Yet robed in thoughtful mortal mien;

And once, no more, the painter's art
Hath touched this mystery on the heart.
Behold her here, untouched by pain
But with foreknowledge of the day
    Still far away
In darkness on the mount of death
Defiled by malefactor's breath—
When " It is finished " he shall cry,
And the immortal seem to die.
Finished? nay, but just begun
    Beneath the sun.
Look at him here a child to-day.

ENGLAND was merry in old times? Indeed!
 When the worn ploughman might not leave the
  ground
Where he was born, and where his children found
His old shoes and nought else for all their need;
When " Benefit of Clergy " saved the deed
 Of blood from punishment, and once a year
 Men climbed a greasy pole for Christmas cheer,
And once in twelve months got one plenteous feed.

Merry in sooth! Astronomy was then
Astrology, the chemist's craft again
 Was alchemy, and every crone grown old
Died as a witch, and you or I, sad fate!
 Had given to fat Mass John our scantiest gold
For his old gown to mask us at heaven's gate!

I.

SAINT DOMINIC.

SAINT Dominic had a vision : Mary mild
   Stood by him shining in her robes of light,
  And warned him fire and sword, the law of might,
Should spread the faith and worship of her child.
Time passed, and holy Church the faggots piled.
  In Italy, in fair Provence, in Spain,
  Prayer was torn up with groans, blood fell like
    rain,
Pity and brotherhood thenceforth exiled.

And I too had a vision of the night :
Appalled by shrieks I rose awake ! red light
  Burst from a pit of fire, and far down there,
While those still rang like a dom-church bell,
  I saw a carcase in the quivering lair :
Dominic it was in Dante's fieriest cell.

II.

TORQUEMADA.

I ROSE in bed, repeated like a child
   The dear Lord's prayer ; a candle lit, and read
The Sermon on the Mount, until my head
Sank on the pillow ; then too soon beguiled
By the same fever-sleep, again the wild
   Horror of death-by-fire, eternally
   Prolonged, possessed my senses, and the cry
Rang up, the shrieks returned ; around me coiled
   That vision of the pit, the pit of doom,
   Where two still living corpses now consume,
Struggling together with their talons thrust
Into each others eye-holes filled with dust.
   'Twas Torquemada in the maddening gloom,
   And Dominic, struggling in their murderous lust.

I.

GOOD, learned, wise, in some sense ; but to-day
   Can we accept a Christopher, poor knight,
  For guide, or take his lanthorn for the light
To guide our pathway, and so shunt away
Whole centuries with their severe assay
   Of all the past ; as if dark night were kin
   To Christian wisdom, and the soul within
Was lost when powerful knowledge holdeth sway ?

Can we ignore our birthright, on the back
   Of packhorse can we seek the dead monk's cell,
   And by the rush-wick in the thick fish-oil,
Let subtle Thomas and Duns Scotus rack
   Our brains till common night-wind seems a coil
Of devils, and we trust some mad old spell !

Ignorance is the curse of God,
Knowledge the wing wherewith we fly to heaven.—Henry VI., Part 2,
  Act iv.

II.

GOOD Newman? well! he gives the devil his
due,
   Honours the Pope, whose chartered power can save
   Gnostics like him on t'other side the grave,
If they but trust nought else, resign all clue
God-given through nature, holding only true
   Traditional Rites, and with sealed eyes contrive
   To shut out reason from their cloistered hive,
And what our mighty science teaches new.

But are they not right happy to have found
   This haven? Ask the smile their thin lips feign
   When workers tell of all the toils and fears
Manhood exacts each step of stable ground.
   Ask the brave triumphs, the material gain
   To civilization for a thousand years.

THE SICKLE.

I.

REACH the old Sickle from the wall
    Where it hath hung so long.
The reaper's re-awakening song
Sounds the autumn's annual call,
Bewildering the watchful hare
In his yet unhunted lair.
Dear old Sickle, once again
The undergrowth of poppies red,
Whose beauties on themselves were shed,
Shall dazzle soon the trembling air,
When the wheat-ears over head
Across thy curved blade have lain,
In triumph as the reaper's eye
Smiles to his fair mate jocundly.

Sacred old Sickle, while the wind
Died on the winter's crisped rind,
And the mossed thatching o'er the door
Was whiter than now is the mill's white floor,
Thou broughtest July's sun to mind:

And so, when May-day breezes blew,
And made each building bird renew
The search for straws and sticks, 'twas thou
For whom we blessed the fledgeling bough,
Then through high summer's long bright eves
Sat the dear saint Tranquility,
Longing to see them gild the sheaves,
And, bread-rich Sickle, glance on thee
Over the villager's shoulder flung,
Love-making fieldward, blythe and young.

II.

Most potent sun, how beautiful
Old harvest days have been,
With health and peace, the garner full,
The fields more yellow than green ;
When upwards thrown on the arch that leaps
        The fly-frequented stream,
Where the tired midday traveller sleeps,
        Danced ever-more the ripple's gleam,
And on its ledge a white-haired child
Sat for idling hours beguiled,

THE SICKLE.

Peeping down right cautiously
A glimmering water friend to see
Smiling from beneath, with hair
Like his own but still more fair.
Beside him laid the bunch of grain,
His earnings in the gleaning train
Then seen through hedge-rows here and there,
Gay in their sun-bright rustic dress,
Where the binder rears the sheaves
At intervals in grouped caress,
Joking wisely as he leaves
Each rustling girth of fruitfulness,
And the looped-up damsels go
Far down the field, now fast, now slow,
Now resting in the sultry air,
Or throwing back betimes their hair
As it falls before their eyes
When they stoop or when they rise.

III.

Beloved Sickle, thou hast been
Where lyre or sword were never seen,

THE SICKLE.

And round thee, like the ivy screen
Around a faun's brown knotted hair,
Clung hopes and fears and blessings rare.
  In a warmer clime
  In a distant time
A goddess held thee in her hand
About whose head's immortal band
Were braided ears of bearded corn,
More loved than even the halo borne
By Phœbus or than Dian's horn.
Round this maternal-goddess' shrine
There was a flower-encircled glow
  Of fruitage and of wine,
To her the autumnal overflow
  Was borne with hymns divine.
This goddess is departed now,
No more she guides the timely plough,
  It grides along alone :
No more men light her temple dim,
Aud the consecrating hymn,
Dear Sickle, long hath been thine own.

THE SICKLE.

IV.

The goddess gone ! ah, no more here
But wrapt up with our school-boy gear
Of dactyl and trochee, no more
On this side of the Stygean shore !
The Sickle too, when I was young,
A doleful when, so long ago !
Was polished bright though never sung.
But now alack, it too must go
Among forgotten things too slow
For these our frantic hours of speed :
No more the boast of kirtled maid,
It rusts among the long decayed ;
Nor more, like Ruth, the gleaner need
Stoop her flexile back to-day.
      Make clear the way !
The grand machine with man and steed,
And countless knives and clash of steel,
Passing on its dangerous fray,
  Makes the child run, the old man reel.

THE SICKLE.

Nor there the end, with welcome sway
From prairies vast the steamship braves
The grim Atlantic's mightiest waves,
Filled with grain from that far land.
The farmer turns his eyes away,
The Sickle dropping from his hand

1ST.

SISTER with the crimson crest
And broad wings of every die,
Come ye from the eagle's nest,
On the mountain turrets high,
Or from kissing the lake below
Swimming thus so softly slow?
Round thy folded feet the breeze
Languishes in blissful ease,
Holding his breath for beauty's sake
Till he hath passed thee unawake.
Our father-sun is gone to sea,
Come thou after him with me.

2ND.

Sister, yes, we shall entwine
Our arms and wings, both thine and mine,
Then wait for me, too fast you stray
Adown that steep though golden way
To the far home of yesterday.

Behold ! the messengers are still
Shedding flame on wave and hill ;
Shield me in thy saffron vest,
So may we in its folds be pressed
Together, and together move
Like lovers in their day of love,
With like colour, and like motion,
Across that fearful, glittering ocean.

1ST.

Foot to foot and hand to hand,
Over sea as over land :
Hark, the children on the strand
Are singing at their evening play.
Can you hear them, what they say ?

2ND.

They are too far, too far away :
But still I see them on the sand
Run before the breaking spray,
And I can see the curfew bell

Swinging in the fretted spire,
Lit up in a bright farewell,
Like a pyramid of fire.

1ST.

But now, oh sister, what are these,
So many and so swift, astray
Up hither far from fields and trees?
They dart right through us like a breeze
With forked tails, strange birds are they.

2ND.

Swallows are they following
Our father-sun to a warmer land;
Swallows, swallows, strong of wing,
Seeking Afric's heated sand—
Already they have passed away,
Lost until another spring.

1ST.

Another spring! another year!
But we are only for a day—

Already I am faint with fear.
Behold those fishermen return
Home across the darkening bay,
Their oars give off that ghastly spray
Where the shoreward surf they spurn.

2ND.

For a day, ah well you say
Only for a single day.
      Dank and cold
And shapeless grows thy mantle's fold.
But where art thou? gone, gone from me
Over the wind-swept darkening sea,
Alas, and I must follow thee.

A LAST WALK, IN ILLNESS.

L ET'S close the book, and underneath the blue
     Stepping again where innocent daisies grow,
Sweet daisies the child's playthings long ago ;
Feel the spring wind as then it briskly blew,
And hear as then we heard the shrill curlew ;
     Make friends with the slow cow upon the lea,
     And seated on this height behold the sea.
Dear ancient sights, for me again so new.

The darkening sea, alas ! night comes apace,
     The sun hath touched his cloud-strewn misty goal ;
To-day as every day he wins the race :
Homeward we turn, homeward we still must look
     When Nature, the stern step-dame of the soul,
Closes for evermore life's half-read book.

THE FURTHER SHORE.

L IFE'S half-read book, for we are well aware
 　　We cannot know it to its furthest end :
 But still we hope the coming page may mend
 Its story, and our sun shine out more fair ;
 That infant laughter may light age's care ;
 　　That Good and Evil's ravelled skeins shall blend
 　　In closer harmony like friend with friend,
 And God's love never leave us anywhere.

But now the book is closed, the dusk falls low
 　　Upon the unknown sea : For me no more
 The Pleiades and Bear will shine : I go ;
 　　My unknown home is on the further shore,
 And when my darkened eyes mark nought below
 　　The Mighty Hand shall guide me as before.

E N D.

www.ingramcontent.com/pod-product-compliance
Lightning Source LLC
Chambersburg PA
CBHW020625030726
47497CB00007B/2411